The Voyage of Saint Brendan

The Navigator

Translated by Gerard McNamara

To my Alison

Contents

Acknowledgments

I would like to thank my Alison for encouraging me to publish this work, and then making it happen.

My parents for always being there for me through all my adventures, which may at times appear odd to an outside observer, and always let me have my head.

My Beatrice, Beaty my Border Collie, my walks companion where many a line was polished and ran home to be written.

And my little boy Freeman, he hasn't done much yet, but even a smile is a fine achievement.

Translator's Introduction

The story of the Voyage of Saint Brendan (b. 484 - d. 577), the wandering Irish monk, has been retold, translated, adapted and versified for over a thousand years. Yet, while the journeys of Odysseus, Aeneas and Dante himself still spur translators in gluts, the Saint Brendan voyage in this century is neglected and has dulled as a result. This is not to imply that The Voyage of Saint Brendan is of equal merit to the great epics, however if these works absorb lifetimes, a proportionate effort is surely warranted for this beautiful little flower of early Celtic Christianity.

The earliest extant version of the story is the 9th century Navigatio Sancti Brendani Abbatis written in Latin. From which this translation has been produced. This has of course been rendered competently into English several times, and the voyage even re-enacted. Yet the story often appears a little charmless in English which for an Irish tale, in particular, is unforgivable. The Latin language by virtue of its inflections lends a simple, fluid excellence to the story which English prose struggles to replicate. For this reason I have attempted a verse translation. I have arranged the story into fourteen chapters made up of eight line stanzas closed with a rhyming or near rhyming couplet. These mimic the eight recurring prayer times of the monk's day, as below;

Matins	Night or midnight prayer; also called Vigils or Nocturnes
Lauds	Dawn Prayer (3 a.m.)
Prime	Early Morning Prayer (First Hour, 6 a.m.)
Terce	Mid-Morning Prayer (Third Hour, 9 a.m.)
Sext	Midday Prayer (Sixth Hour, 12 p.m.)
None	Mid-Afternoon Prayer (Ninth Hour, 3 p.m.
Vespers	Evening Prayer (also 'the lighting of the lamps', 6 p.m.)
Compline	Night Prayer (before retiring, 9 p.m.)

A critical factor for any long poem is flow and fluidity, to this end I have used iambic pentameter as the backbeat to the story. Where necessary I have added or taken an extra syllable to moderate the rhythm. Directly rendered Latinisms are sprinkled throughout where appropriate to the tone of the moment, but for the most part the vocabulary is very simple.

Did the historical Saint Brendan undertake such a voyage and even discover the American continent? Was his Hell an Icelandic volcano and his crystal pillar an iceberg? I certainly don't answer these ongoing ponderings over the Brendan voyage here and refer the interested reader to other works that address these aspects of the journey. Rather, this work is born of the frustration at not being able to enjoy an exuberant English translation of this wonderful story.

Chapter 1.   Barinthus' Tale

Saint Brendan – Finlug son of Alte's son,
Navigator, first sprung from Munster's fens
Amongst the Yew-tree-men; the Owens.
A man of great refrain, famed and restless
Laden with virtues, and fatherhood,
Abbot to three thousand holy brethren.

He was there that evening at war again
With battered want, atop his lovely hill,
When a certain Father of King Neil's clan
Came weeping by the sea to Ardfert town.
This Father Barinthus fell down and cried
At each word the Saint did put to him –
Then; his face seemed stuck in numbing prayer
And he stared him through a thousand stares.

Saint Brendan raised the man with calm embrace
Saying to the transfixed face "Father why
Is your arrival such a dismal thing
For us, did you come to consolation bring?
It might serve well, if you did, to cheer somewhat.
Let us know these secrets, these words of God.
Refresh our souls with stories of the sea
And ocean miracles that you have seen."

At this the saintly man did start to move
His lips with luring words for Brendan's ears.
He began to speak of a certain isle:
"My son had fled my sight to live alone
Mernoc, once a man for the poor of Christ
To be a solitary, an anchorite.
Close by the League of Cliffs he did alight
Upon a land - an Island of Delights.

For a long time I never heard a thing;
Then came a bit of news of how he lived.
He was a man of many miracles now
And had scores of monks at his command.
At that I went to visit, and was met
Three days out — by my son and his three friends
Warned by God; we sailed the strait and saw ahead
Swarms of monks like bees all dashing from their dens.

Although they thronged to greet from scattered coves
They were unanimous in faith and hope
And charity, one arena for all
The works of God forever worked as one.
No food but roots and nuts and fruits and greens,
And Compline gone, to each his room alone,
To wait reclined until the cockerel sings
Or prayer bells call them out with distant rings.

I went to bed that night upon the isle
And when the morning came we walked it round,
My son my guide to the dark coast bent
And found a boat to me, saying as he went
"We sail West old man, so get aboard,
We'll wend the seas toward a Land of Saints
Promised to them by God for those to come
Beneath the final blazes of the sun."

We clambered in and pushed away the shore,
Then were rushed upon by a flock of clouds
That joined on every side to blind our view,
So that for an hour or more we hardly saw
Our ship's own stern and prow, then struck a light
That raged as if the sun had burst its heart
Across the sea, a land appeared in white
A fruiting place, a wide and grassy isle.

To earth our boat came sliding to a halt,
And though we walked around the curving shore
For fifteen days we never found its end.
Every plant had flowers and fruit the trees
Sparkling, every stone was a precious gem.
And farther still, another fifteen days
We found a river with an eastwards bend
Falling to the sunrise, tempting us ahead.

We yearned to cross but waited word from God
In doubt we foundered – until suddenly
A certain shining man appeared to us
From within a splendid light, he spoke our names
And said: "Greetings good brothers and well done
For the Lord hath lent unto your eyes this view
His Saint's Land, yet this stream you shall not pass
Turn your backs men, upon this other half."

When he paused we asked from where he came
And of his name; but he said: "Why talk of that?
How is it you ask me not about the isle
Which hath stood thus since God began the world?
Do tell me: have you need of food or drink?
Know – friends; a full year you have wandered here
Yet you have not had once the urge to eat
Nor felt the gloom of night or weight of sleep."

"Hearken; behold: this isle is never dark
For Christ is this land's ceaseless spring of light."
At that we stood in tears, and faced about
And went towards the shore that moored our boat;
The man of light came with us all the while
Then softened from our sight as we cast away
Through the fog, towards the Island of Delights
Where the brothers flocked with joy upon our sight.

With relief aside the monks did then bemoan:
"Why Fathers, leave your own sheep shepherdless
To stray lost in this forest of distress?
We knew our Abbot often went away
Though exactly where, we could never tell.
But we do know he only stayed a month
Or a week or two – or maybe less
Then straining glances tore for his regress."

On hearing this I tried to comfort them
"Brothers" I said, "think nothing but good things
For the ground on which you pass your way is blessed
It lies in the shadows of the portals
Of Paradise; an isle not far from here
Called the Land of Saints, where night never looms
And morning never fades – this is where he went
Our Mernoc, with Angel guides and God's consent."

"Don't you recall this fragrance on our garbs?
See – we're dubbed by the incense of Paradise."
The monks then answered, "We thought as much
That he went to the Paradise of God
But where in the wide sea we never knew.
For forty days afterwards of his return
We did notice that same Godly scent
Lacing the breeze with blissful redolence."

For two more weeks I stayed there with my son,
During which time we fasted scrupulously
Yet, we felt fuller than when we did begin.
So complete was our satiety
Corporeally, we seemed to all replete.
And after forty days I left that place
With the Abbot's grace, I sailed the swells
Where by morn I'll trek towards my little cell."

Chapter 2.   The Monks Depart

Barinthus' words sent Brendan to the floor,
With all his congregation felled to earth
Glorying in God they chanted out:
"O Lord, thou art righteous in all thy ways
Holy are thy works – and this glimpse for us
Thy slaves, of such and so great a wonder;
Be blessed for this boon thou hast today bestowed
This delicious morsel - this supernal goad."

With the song's surcease Saint Brendan rose and said:
"Let us now refresh our bodies with food
We'll nourish the new commandment as we chew."
And by this repast the night-time passed to morn
So they blessed Barinthus and he left for home.
Whereupon Saint Brendan set to work;
He picked fourteen of his most loyal men
Then in an oratory he secluded them.

"My faithful soldiers" he said, "listen here
I need some help, and your advice sincere,
For every thought and all of my desires
Have joined in force, and now they do conspire
Upon my will with one devouring urge –
To set out now upon the rolling surge
And if God wills, to find this Land of Saints,
This virgin muse of all good Barrind's claims."

"Well – what do you think, what do you say?"
But knowing full their saintly father's heart
They answered almost all as one, "Father
Your aim is ours – whatever it may be.
We cast off our parents and their wills for you;
Renounced our very bodies to your care
So, if this the Lord as much as you does move
Then off to death or life - take us as you do."

Thereupon, Brendan, and those to sail with him
Thought wise to make a fast of forty days
For three days at a time, before leaving shore.
Then with this complete, and keener by its wear
The Saint farewelled the monks who were to stay
And commended them to their new abbot's care.
Wherewith he struck the sea, and with strokes they sailed
Westwards to the isle from where Saint Enda hailed.

For three days and nights they abode that place;
Brendan was blessed by the whole monastery.
Then he travelled to the most distant part
Of his homeland, where his parents lived,
However, he did not wish to see them.
Instead, on a spur that dug into the sea
Saint Brendan's Seat – he stopped and fixed a tent
Near a stream, starved, for but a lone boat's breadth.

There they set with tools of iron to make their skiff,
Lightly sprung with wicker ribs and trim
Such as they fashion in those parts of Eire;
Covered all up with ox-hide tanned in oak.
They smeared the joints with lard, packing skins for spares
For two more boats and food for forty days,
With extra grease to plaster all that hide
They packed sundry things for life upon the brine.

Then they raised the mast and hung the sail;
Saint Brendan ordered the brothers aboard
In the name of the Father and of the Son
And of the Holy Spirit – but while he stood
Alone on the shore to bless the scanty bay
There – three monks from his old abbey appeared,
They traced his tracks, grovelling at his feet
And beseeched their father's footprints with their pleas.

"Father, free us to follow at your heels
Or we will die, right here, on this shore
Of hunger and thirst for we are fixed
To lead travelling lives," and so they begged
And when the man of God saw their resolve
He hurried them aboard saying as they went
"Let your wills be done my little sons
But know," he added, "that I know why you've come."

"One of you is honest and for that the Lord
Has reserved a happy place aboard,
But, for the other two the news is grim
It seems that God has only death booked in."
At that, Saint Brendan climbed into the boat
He spread the sail which gathered up the wind;
And they set their course with straining bolsters
Towards the beaming throne; the summer solstice.

They were blessed with such a prosperous breeze
That there was nothing to be done but sit
And trim the sail for fifteen easy days.
Then the wind ceased and they took straight to their oars
And rowed until they were defunct with fatigue;
At which Saint Brendan soothed them with his words
And admonishment, saying, "Brothers don't
Be scared, for God himself is aboard this boat."

"He is mariner, mate and helmsman all
So relax and let your oars and rudder fall,
Leave the sail as it's set, for God will do
As he wills - with this his boat, and servant crew."
And by evening's Vespers and their daily bread
They often felt a friendly night-breeze blow,
Yet, from which quart it loosed they never knew
Nor, to which paths it heft their bark pursue.

After forty days of this, spent and gone
With all their victuals teased to crumbs
An island appeared to their northern side.
It reared so rocky and lofted high
That when they came alongside its banks
They were faced with cliffs and bursting waterfalls,
Rivulets running water to the sea
Sweet down jagged sides from laden peaks.

Yet, this land showed no port to breach its walls
So that the monks, famished and vexed with thirst,
In their despair reached out with their jugs
To capture some drink from those tumbling wells;
"What a foolish thing to do," said Brendan
"An act I would never wish on you,
For God has not yet shown to us the way
To an inlet where our boat can safely lay."

"Do you wish to seem pirates to our Lord?
Don't fear, for Jesus will show us to our port
In but three days we'll be at rest ashore."
So; for three more days they circled round the isle
Then at three o'clock by the Psalms of None
They spied a cleft through which a boat might squeeze;
And between the mighty jambs they drove their skiff
Into a loch – within the cloven cliff.

At once ashore Saint Brendan praised the sight
And told the men to take nothing from the boat.
Then they spotted scampering in the far,
A little dog, on a sea-shore path
Rushing to meet them, he ran to Brendan's feet
Obedient as if at his master's heel.
 "What a charming little guide that God has sent,
Laughed the saint – "let us follow to where he wends."

So, close upon the pads of their canine scout
Saint Brendan and all his brotherly crew
Came to the grounds of a magnificent hall,
Bedecked throughout its mansion length with beds
And couches all laid out; chairs and basins too
Filled with water, fresh to wash their holy feet.
"Beware," warned Brendan as the monks reclined
"That Satan should tempt you with what you find."

"I see that one of our latest three
Shall apprentice with Satan - as a thief,
To thieve wickedly in bedevilled flesh;
So pray for his soul – for the meat's putresced."
And they saw in the house they rested in
The walls adorned, with bridles and bugles,
Vases flashing all the metals of the earth
With cornets flush in silver round their girdles.

Then Brendan asked the Monk of the Meals
Who apportioned bread to his brothers
To bear to them the lunch that God had sent.
At which the man went straightaway and found
A dining table already set
With a table cloth and a place for all,
To which for each, a piece of bread - shining white
Had been allotted with a fish beside.

With the food arrayed Saint Brendan praised the lunch
"Let us all," he said, "laud beyond the skies
For He who caters thus from heaven's heights"
Therefore they sat glorifying God
And they came upon such volumes of drink
That with half a part they drenched their thirsts.
Then with the works of God and of want complete
Saint Brendan ushered off the men to sleep.

"To rest! and look, you each have a ready bed
Well made to relieve your leadened arms and legs
Weary by the weight of our great fatigue
So, go men – feast now upon your dues of sleep."
And over the slumbering monks Brendan watched
And saw the Devil through an eyelid's chink,
Cavorting as an Ethiopian child
With a laughing monk and a stolen bridle.

The Saint got out of bed at once, and prayed,
Withstanding his vigil by nocturnes of grace
Until the morning when the Brothers woke
And hurried to complete the work of God,
So that they could hasten to their waiting boat.
But there, before them – a furnished table
Just as they were set to the day before,
And with which would be blessed for three days more.

Chapter 3.   The Island of the Giant Sheep

After this, and urged back out to sea
The saint said to the brothers, "Listen men,
Look while you leave to take nothing from this isle."
To which in turn they cried, "Father – God forbid
That any theft should violate our voyage."
"But behold – this monk, just as I forebode
Who holds in his habit's folds the silver bit
Which last night the Devil tacked him with."

And at that, the brother hurled the bridle
Down from his bosoms hold and sunk cowered
To the feet of his master, the man of God.
"Father I am guilty" - he begged - "please forgive
My ruined soul, and pray that I might live?"
At this they fell, prostrating themselves,
His blood and friends to the earth entreating
The Lord for the soul of their brother pleading.

Standing then – all leavened from the earth,
The guilty monk by the saintly father,
They saw burst forth from the heaving breast
A crazed and shrieking Ethiopian
Howling at the shock, "Why by God do you strike
Me from my home of seven years, and worse
Estrange me from my hereditary right?"
To which Saint Brendan heaved his words of might.

"I tell you now – by our Lord Jesus Christ
Never to no man more attempt entice
Hence now until the judgment day arrives."
And turning then to the erring monk
"Take up the body and the blood of Christ
For your soul will leave your body now to die;
This is your gravesite, your final cell.
Better than the brother next, who dies in hell."

So the man took up the Eucharist;
Then his soul was spilled out from its hold
Lifted by an angel lit for all to see,
While the saintly father buried the corpse
To lie at the very place where they all stood.
Then away they went towards the shore
Where - boarding ship, a youth came down to them
With a basket full of amphorae and bread.

"Take this blessing" he said, "by the hand
Of your friend, for a long way still remains
Until you shall discover consolation.
Yet all the while you'll not stomach deficience
Of bread or water till the dawn of Easter."
So they took this blessing with themselves to sea
And thither and across the world of waves
They ate their fare to spare each second day.

At last they came within an island's view
Not long away, so they bent their oars
And in the reach some helpful bellows blew
So they hadn't need to labour past their strength.
Then, with their boat settled firmly in its port
The man of God told his men to set forth
As he himself stepped out to lead his crew
With feet to feed their eyes the arching view.

With the rounding of the isle they saw en masse
Its liquid largesse - flowing in streams
From fountains and pools filled with teeming fish.
Saint Brendan said to his brotherly crew,
"Let us, right here, perform our work divine
We'll sacrifice the spotless lamb in time
For our Lord's Last Supper," and there they stayed
Until the feast of Holy Saturday.

Then they walked and searched about the isle
Finding meadows grassed with lawns of fleece
For flocks roamed throughout of perfect coloured sheep
All white – packed so woven tight to blank the earth.
At this sight Saint Brendan convoked his crew,
"Pluck from this flock what you need for the feast."
And at this command from the man of God
The brothers hurried off towards the flock.

They took a single creature from the fold
And bound it by the horns - but it followed led
Placidly as if long tamed to men;
With slack in hand they walked it to the Saint
Who said to one of them, "Now go back
Take from the flock one lamb immaculate."
This was quickly done by the one ordained
As they all prepared to feast the coming day.

While doing so, a man appeared beside
Holding a basket filled, amongst all else,
With bread cakes, baked from underneath the fire.
He laid this down before the man of God
Then sunk himself, face first to the feet
Of his saintly father falling three times,
"By what grace did I earn that the Pearl of God
Should taste this Easter the labours of my plot?"

Saint Brendan raised him and kissed him, saying,
"My son, it was our Lord Jesus Christ
Who proposed that here we might rejoice his life
And resurrection," - but the man replied
"Today, father, you shall celebrate here
But for tomorrow's rites and holy Mass
The Lord suggests that isle in yonder view
Lies best to feast His rise - and death's rebuke."

While he spoke, he was seized in compliance
With every will of the servants of God
And ceaselessly replenished their supplies,
Which he hauled aboard saying to the Saint,
"Your vessel can now not carry one thing more
So, on Pentecost, I'll bring you further stores."
"But how will you know" Saint Brendan asked
"Where to find us after eight days passed?"

"Tonight you'll rest on this island by my shores
Until tomorrow noon when you will part
To a land, not far, in the western seas
Which they call the Paradise of the Birds,
There you shall remain until the Octave
Of Pentecost." Saint Brendan then inquired
How there came to be such giant sheep
On the isle as big it seemed as burden's beasts.

"No one ever milks them here" the man replied
"Nor does winter strain them with tufts of fare,
Instead they linger idly about the glens
At roam amongst the pastures night and day
For that, they are much larger than in your parts."
With this said they set out once more for their boat
And as the ocean swept between crew and host
They vied to bless – from each the other most.

Chapter 4.   Jasconius and the Paradise of Birds

As they neared the bankments of the island
They grazed a strand which beached their boat offshore
And standing firmly; harbourless at sea
Saint Brendan told the men to leave the craft.
Which they did - putting ocean to their feet.
Then both the beams they fastened with a rope
And through the water waded with the cord,
Pausing, only when they paused within their port.

The island was a stoned and grassless place
With sandless coasts and flotsam-wooded range
Yet, inland went the monks to pass the night
To pray and stay awake before the Lord.
Away from the boat where the Saint remained
For well he knew what sort the island was,
But didn't wish to sound aloud his fears
Lest they terrify completely when they hear.

In the dawn the priests were asked to sing,
Each besought to make his Mass in song,
And while the Saint himself was carolling
Still in the boat; the men began to work
Hauling raw meat to cure and fish to salt
Brought from the other isle, tumbled in their pot;
But when they ministered firewood to the flames
It took - and the whole isle shook them like a wave.

They raced in panic off towards the boat
Begging for help from their saintly father
Who took each by the hand and dragged him in.
They managed to sail but relinquished all their gear
As the island travelled onwards out to sea.
For two more miles they could see their fire
A flame, on its way, as they heard the Saint
Explain to them the truth about the place.

"Brothers – are not any of you surprised
At what this land has just done before your eyes?"
"No, indeed: we were too much amazed
Then terrified sick, now – paralysed."
 "My sons" he said, "don't become afraid
For last night God himself to me conveyed,
Revealing by a sacred vision,
The mystery of this expedition."

"That was not an island - but a fish
First and greatest of all the swimming things
It forever tries to join its tail and head
But can never make them meet with such a length,
For that they call him Jasconius."
As he spoke they'd rounded on their tracks
And drifting by the isle where they'd passed three days
They found by its western shores a narrow strait.

Across the sound they saw another land
Lush of grass and forested with flowers.
So, they circled round its shores to find a port
And instead a rivulet, by its southern banks
Running to the sea, here they sent their craft.
And Brendan asked the crew then disembarking
To drag the boat with ropes against the bed
Beneath the stream that barely held their breadth.

With their holy father sitting in the skiff
They dragged their burden for a mile upstream
To the fountain spring of that very creek.
And there Saint Brendan thought and said, "Behold;
What a place that Christ our Lord has placed us by
To rest and remain during this Easter time.
And I believe - that were we short supplied
This font would well our every need provide."

But by them hung a disconcerting sight –
A tree of marvellous bole but stunted height
That was wholly overwhelmed with shining birds
So that its feathered branches and white downed leaves
Were behind its brilliant cover hardly seen.
This sight plunged the saint deep within himself
As he trolled his mind for the whats and why
Such a multitude of birds would there alight.

Yet all he netted was grief, and splashed with tears
Frustrated with himself he went to knees
Self deprecating to entreat the Lord,
"My God – knower of the unknown
And revelator of the shrouded shown,
Only you discern the torment in my heart;
Deign then, great mercy, to a sinner tell
What secrets before these very eyes do well."

"I ask with no thought of worth or merit
Just begging hope of your mighty clemence."
And with this said, all within, and calmed again
One of the birds alit from its perch
And swooped with plumes that rang like little bells
To light by the beam where the Saint was held.
And high on the prow she spread her placid wings
Signing joy and gazed at the Saint within.

Saint Brendan knew at once that God had heard
And recorded his hearts supplication
So he spoke to the bird, "Herald of God
If that is who you are, tell me please for what
Or from where, these birds come now collected here."
She replied at once "We come out of ruin;
From the great and ancient smiting of the fiend
That trapped us, drowned, in Satan's plunging reach."

"But our God is a true and righteous lord;
His sentence was to send us to this world
Where we sustain no pain but the space of Him
Whose closeness is kept for those of greater faith.
We are peregrines free in this airy land
To wander, spirits, the firmament or ground,
Except for feasts or Sundays made for praise
When we are as you see with such bodies graced."

"And you, with your brothers are one year gone
In this journey there are still six more to come.
Today – where you toasted the Paschal feast
So will you there each of the coming years.
Then you will find what you've set in your heart
This promised land, Paradise of the Saints."
Then with this, she went up from off the prow
And found her place among the blazing crowd.

With the lighting of the lamps then falling near
The birds began to beat their sides and sing
"In Zion songs of praise adore Thee Lord
The vow is paid in Jerusalem to God."
An hour they looped and circled round the Psalm,
And to the Saint and those that went with him
Those chanting throats and softly humming wings
Made sounds as like the sweetest beaten hymns.

Thereupon Saint Brendan said to his crew
"Now feed your limbs, for God has sated
Our craving souls with his divine creations."
Then with supper's end and the Compline prayer
Came the command to take them off to slumber.
They slept until the third vigil of the night
When the man of God awaking woke his men
And "*Open my lips Lord,*" off to vigil went.

All the birds resounded - mouth and wing
With *"Praise the Lord"* to Brendan's midnight din
"Adore his power - all the angels sing."
And so they passed the night-times wrapped in song.
With Aurora flashing-back before the sun
"O may Thou splendid be" and on they sung
By Psalms of measured beats and melodies
With the twilight prayer in just equality.

At Terce they chanted *"Sing to our God our King"*
At Sext in song *"Shine Thy face on sin"*
For None in Psalms *"Behold the good begun
How fine it is for Brethren blent to one."*
In such a way by day and night they worked
The birds to render praise up to their Lord;
Accordingly, the Saint refreshed his men
And thus the Easter fete and Octave spent.

Chapter 5. The Three Fountains

The feast days therefore ended with the order:
"Receive your stipends, brothers, of this water;
For until now it has not felt our need
But when by rite we washed our hands and feet."
And with these words the foresaid man appeared
With whom they all had spent three Easter days;
He that lavished tributes on the crew
Came overflowing in his boat with food.

He produced it all, the volume of his lot
Right before his saintly father's feet
"Brothers and men – here you have food to last
Until the sacred day of Pentecost,
But watch the fountain – for it's strong to drink
Heavily drugged from its depthless spring,
And who would try would feel such rush of sleep
That he could not wake the day he drunk for each."

"As long as they flow from such a stream
These brooklets swell with lethargy and dreams."
At this, the man betook of being blessed
By the father, and returned from whence he went.
Saint Brendan stayed there until Pentecost
For the birds revived them so much with their songs;
And while the Saint and his family sung their Mass
Their provider came again with full repast.

As they sat to lunch the man partook of speech,
"A long way still remains for you of this -
So take from this fountain your flagons full
This dry bread too, which can years endure;
And of these loaves I'll leave you such supplies
Your boat will not a basket more abide."
Then this complete the man again took leave
And went home with all the blessings he'd received.

Eight days later Saint Brendan filled the boat
With all their cargo rationed by their host
And ranged the pitchers sparkling from the well,
Then, leading all the men towards the coast
That bird roused herself, that formerly had spoke.
She flew with speed and re-sat upon the prow;
Apprising to the saint without a word
Her wish at their departure to be heard.

With human voice the bird began to talk
"We'll see you all again at this place next year
To pass the time that you've passed with us here;
And where you were for the Lord's last feast
There - with your past before you'll always be
And at the same time but the year between,
So too for the Vigil, first and then
Upon Jasconi's back again and again."

"Yet, even so – you shall discover too
By the Nativity of the Lord
The island order of Saint Ailbey's men
And Christmas there after eight months voyage."
Then she paused and winged away to sing –
As the wind astern caught fading wisps of hymn
And with far-off songs they laboured through the sea
The hope of earth and ruin of the deep."

And thus the saintly father with his crew
Strayed the widths of long and lengths of latitude,
Cast for three months to the violence of the main
And void of sight, but for heaven and the waves.
On every third or second day they supped
Until land reared close and fast upon their side;
But as they neared still closer to the coast
An adverse wind caught and held their weary boat.

They were hauled for forty days around the isle
Weak in dreams of land and reachless shores;
So the sea-borne brothers, desperate, begged their Lord
For help – weeping with their wilting strength
Which by this lassitude was nearly slaught;
They persevered in constant prayer and fast,
And in three days an inlet showed its face
All anguished but for a single passageway.

There seemed to flow two fountains from its head
One fell turbid - the other clear and fresh
So the brothers hurried onwards with their cups
While the watching Saint stood hopeless to refrain -
"My sons, do not think of carrying through with this
An illicit act made with rude remiss
For the license and the seniority
Of these holy men and elders of the sea."

"They'll present, I'm sure, spontaneously
More than your furtive thirst could ever thieve."
Then with this he went down from off the boat
And while he thought to where they all should go
A man of great age and gravity arose
With a face of clarity and glowing hair
He kissed the saint and bowed three times so low
That all the men had to lift him off the road.

Then with welcome kisses dutifully exchanged
The old man, steadied by the hand of the Saint,
Walked them a mile to the monastery's grounds
Where before the gates Saint Brendan asked,
"Whose place is this – what Abbot here presides
Tell me brother, from where they've all arrived?"
And with varied sermons Brendan did enquire
But could not wrest an answer with his wiles.

Rather, with incredible gentleness
The ancient brother hinted with a sign;
Which the holy father saw at once
Bidding his men with a warning quick
"Keep custody of your words my crew
Lest your scandalous mouths these men abuse"
In their way stood eleven brothers singing
With cases and relics and crosses swinging.

"Arise, Saint, from your abode, and set out
For truth – to bless this abbey and its men
Your servants, deign, with shields of peace defend."
At song's end their Father came to kiss the Saint
To which monk to monk they made their signs of peace;
Then led in prayer, as is done in western parts
Antiphons sounded the commandment new
And feet were washed, *"That now I give to you."*

The singing ended with a great silence
Through which they were led towards the hall.
There, they bathed their hands and a sign was beaten
Then seated - a second signal rung
Forcing to his feet one of the abbey's men
Who sped forthwith to administer the bread,
He brought it forward glaring in its white,
With roots of shining sweetness by their side.

Then by order mingled – monk to guest
They sat, and to each pair a bread was put;
Then the same man at the signal's urging
Brought to each brother the drinking pot
And as the monks all drank amongst themselves
With great hilarity the Abbot taunted
"Drink boys, with joy and the fear of God
From the font you wished today to rob."

"And from the muddy one, we reserve for guests
We give you now with charity and gladness;
Though indeed; we use it but to wash our feet,
For it's daily warmed by some secret heating.
As for all this shining bread you see
We know not the baker nor the kiln
Nor even he who ports the load itself
It just appears - upon our cellar shelves."

"But come – the Master is of course the Lord
Who ministers these eleemosynary serves
By some creature obedient to his word
Bringing two dozen monks one dozen breads,
And on feast days and Sundays one apiece
Enough to dine on but the crumbs themselves.
Just now double rations on your arrival
God bearing burden of our survival."

"So it has happened these eighty years
Since Saint Patrick's day and the time of Ailbey
Yet, extreme age or languor is yet to term
If not to part us, and rigor up our limbs.
We never eat by fire nor fever strike
Kept warm too by the lights of our homeland -
Brought for Mass by divine predestination
And burning wickless since our fold's foundation."

Chapter 6.   Saint Ailbey's Isle

Three rounds later the evening tolls were sounded
As is custom there every brother rose
Grave and silent marching to the doors,
All in matching steps before their masters.
In this way they shuffled to the church
And seemed with plunging genuflections
To have somehow reflected off the walls
As likewise returned twelve other brothers more.

"Abbot" – asked the Saint, referring to the sight
"Why did these men not dine with us tonight?"
"Don't fear" the host replied, "they will eat
And would well have refreshed themselves before
But that for guests, our table is too small.
Now, let's step into the church ourselves
It's the hour of Vespers, and when we've sung
Those monks can theirs when their time is rung."

Once they'd paid off all their vesperal debts
Saint Brendan took at once to considering
How and with what this edifice was built.
It was square indeed, with matching lengths
And widths, all lit by seven lanterns
Set two by two, and three by the altar
Which was made of solid crystal, squarely cut
As was the paten, chalice and pouring jugs.

Each piece pertaining to worship divine
Was wrought like, of clear quartz and crystalline.
And making a circuit of the church's walls
Were the two choirs and their four and twenty stalls
Each beginning at the other's pause
There and again at the chair of their father.
Only he intoned to initiate their songs
Or ever dared to speak amongst the flock.

In the monastery no voice or sound
Or utterance was ever to be heard
If some monk needed some necessary thing
He could, genuflecting, face his father
And ask him with the spirit of his heart,
Or by signs; to which, written justice
On a tablet dictated by the Lord
The Abbot bore the findings to his ward.

As Saint Brendan pondered on the Order;
Reviewing all that he'd seen, the Abbot spoke
"Father, now we go again to the hall
To do all we can before the twilight falls."
Then, like the shadows of their lunch, they dined
Completing, with Compline, the day's demands
In perfect order, they worked to fill their vows
As their Abbot toned the foretold lines aloud.

In awe of the Holy Trinity they sung
"Hasten Lord to help us – evil ones
Spare us, who iniquity have done
To sleep well and rest in peace itself,
For only you bear hope in us our Lord."
After this they chanted for the hour
Then outside to fresh air and on to their cells
With each indweller taking a guest as well.

Inside the church the captains both remained
Watchful – waiting for the coming of the light
In the quietness Saint Brendan asked
How a regime of such total silence
Could ever be endured by human life,
With great reverence the Abbot replied
"I humbly confess Father some eighty years
Have seen us living on this island here."

"Except for songs and praises of the Lord
We have never heard a voice but that of yours.
These men of mine are never moved to more
Than finger signs or motions of the eye
And only the oldest are so endorsed.
Here we are never sought by illness
Or savaged by the sickness of the mind
That circles, awaiting the waste of mankind."

"Can it be that we should have leave to stay?"
Saint Brendan asked at the Abbots speech
"No, Father, you do not have leave;
It is not at all the will of God;
Why do you ask – haven't you been told
Before you set out for this far-flung isle,
That with fourteen of your loyal crew aside
You are to turn to home one day to die?"

"Of your men only two of them will stay,
One destined to wander from his brothers' way
And in the land of the anchorites remain;
The other is condemned, disgraced and lost
A guest forever in the house of hell."
Then as they spoke, they saw burst forth
A flaming arrow – flashing through the jambs
Igniting, as it passed, the altar lamps.

The arrow was at once outside and gone
Outstayed in its brilliance as the altar shone
Forcing Blessed Brendan to words again,
"Father, who extinguishes the morning lights?"
"Come and see the secret yourself," he replied
"Behold – candles, in their holders burning
But look, they are never really burning down
For these are by flames of a spirit crowned ."

Then Saint Brendan asked how it could be
"That in a corporeal creature such light
Incorporeal, corporeally brightened?"
The old man replied, "Haven't you ever heard
Of Mount Sinai and the burning bush
That left the thicket yet inviolate?"
And thus they thought and in the vigil spoke
Through all the night until the brothers woke.

In the sunrise Saint Brendan petitioned
For leave to set out once more on his voyage
But was with "Father" by the man denied
"You must celebrate Christmas here with us
Until the Octave of the Epiphany."
He stopped therefore, the saintly father
With his crewmen for the ordered time
Alongside the brothers of Saint Ailbey's Isle.

Chapter 7.   The Brothers Indulge

After all the Christmas feasts had passed
With gifts of blessings, borne with drinks and bread
The blessed Brendan – that saintly man
Went with his followers down towards the shore.
Where, sails spread he quickly fled to sea
Navigating however and wherever –
And whether by oars or the wind was sent
To many nameless places until Lent.

This is when Saint Brendan saw the island
And when the brothers caught the sight themselves
Huge-eyed with three days of failed stores
They vanished, set by hunger and thirst
From beside themselves, throwing back the surf;
And landed – rowing, they waited for the Saint
To bless the bay and free them from the boat
Which they exited directly as he spoke.

Their first sight was water falling clear
Flawless – the most lucid fountain of their trip,
And in a circuit thriving by its falls
Were roots and herbs, incessant in their sorts,
In its currents too – every piscine breed
Went running through to the hollows of the sea,
So the Saint remarked, in reverence of the isle;
"God has given comfort to our trial."

"Let us roast these fish upon a fire
Take just as many as the meals require,
Collect from the gardens too of roots and herbs
Which God has prepared, for us to serve."
Thus it was done, to which the man of God
Having sipped the stream to test the spring
"And Brothers, beware you don't go too far
And the enjoyment of this well surpass."

"Weigh the words of all our warnings too
Lest too heavily they fall on you."
But the brothers partook unequally
In the interpretation of this decree
Each giving his own consideration
To the advice of the man of God,
Some drank one cup and others two apiece
While the rest judged less at three cups each.

Great stupor weighed at once upon them all –
And they buckled with amazement to the floor,
The worst collapsed for three days and three nights
With their fallen brothers lost for two beside,
And in fair proportion to the taken cups
The first, a half condemned, again woke up.
All the while befallen their Father prayed
To amend this ignorance his men displayed.

When they'd slept, with three days cast away
The saintly father said to the brethren
"Brothers, get up quick and flee your deaths
Before worse befalls your heavy heads;
God in goodness to pasturage laid us
But you ravished it and wrought it fatal.
So go – and in departing hasten
To leave at once this ruinous haven."

"Take with you however many fish you need
To eat but one day of every three,
Enough to last till the Lord's last feast,
Get water too, a cup a man a day
Similarly of the roots along the way."
They took at once the orders of the Saint
And with laden boat and tautened veil
Through the ocean to the North seas sailed.

Three days later all their wind was stopped
And the ocean seemed to quiet and congeal
Becoming as if impenetrable
Then too smooth and excessively tranquil,
In the calm Saint Brendan told his crew,
"It's God's watch now and our work intrudes;
So remit the oars and the cloth relax
For while God is Captain – all is act."

For twenty days they moved by varied places
And when through all those whereabouts were brought
The breeze of God awakened to their course,
Always rushing East towards the dawn;
So they stretched their sail high up to the wind
And twice-weekly gave refreshments to themselves
Until an island seeming like a cloud
Appeared upon the air above their bow.

"Sons, do you recall that island over there"
The men replied that they did not at all
"But yet" he told them in return "I do
It's where last year we served the Lord's last meal
That land our goodly procurator fields."
The crew responded instantly with rowing
And fervent in their joyfulness they strained
With as much as all their power could sustain.

 "Little fools – don't wear your tiny limbs"
The man of God decried, on seeing this
"Is not God commander of the ship;
He is all-powerful and sails well
So let Him guide us by these island swells."
And as the seaboard clarified in closing
Their steward with his curragh seized their course
To land as they'd left the year they came before.

Praising God he stayed his boat and kissed them
Starting with the saintly father's feet
"God is most wonderful in his Saints"
And *"Blessed be God"* with the crew's most novice;
Then on to toil, his versicle completed
He took them all in tow from off their boat
To where he put a tent upon the shore
And in the pools their bathing waters poured.

It was indeed the Lord's last supper
To which the man produced them all new clothes
And for the next three days he served the crew
In absolute obedient travail.
The brothers likewise immortalised
With transfixed minds the Passion of the Lord,
And sacrificing victims as their God
They marked each one the Holy Sabbath's lot.

With supper closed their procurator spoke
Saying to the Saint and those that went along
"Now proceed, and go up in your boat
To celebrate this sacred Sunday's eve –
Staying witness to the rising day
Atop of where you went the other year,
Hold – until the sun acclaims its crown
And gained, depart, aloft that blazing hour."

"Travel then towards the other island
The one they call the Paradise of Birds
That where last year you rested by the well
Until the Octave of Pentecost."
They set at once to carry out this bidding
While the man himself took straightway to their ship
And with food and flesh and drinks and bits
Made onerous capacity with it.

Saint Brendan gave return of benedictions
Ascending to his place within the craft
He took at once to steering to the island.
And coming near to where they soon must stand
Their pot appeared the year before abandoned,
So leading with a hymn he left the boat
And singing the Song of the Three Young Men
Conduced his chanting brothers to the end.

"Watch and pray" he warned at the songs completion
"And heed enter not into temptation
For look well what God has put beneath our feet
This floating brute, most massive of the sea."
The brothers therefore to prayers disbanded
And strewn in their vigils on the isle
From evening till the night's abatement
Each the dawn's arising pageant waited

Every priest sung in rank his service
And at the third hour of the morning Mass
The man of God killed the shining lamb
Speaking as he did to his brethren
"We feted thus last Holy Sunday here
And thus the same I wish this very year."
To which forthwith proceeding on his words
They parted to the Island of the Birds.

Chapter 8. The Sea Beasts Battle

Voyaging to the other island's shore
The birds in waves of concord sent their song
"Eternity to our God upon his throne
And to the Lamb; for the Lord most high
Who gave us day – anoint a feast of sun
The altar plunged in shadows to the rungs"
And with trilling throats and purring wings
The half an hour blurred into the hymn.

So the saintly father with his saintly crew
With all aboard employed in getting forth
Left and in their tent upon the shore
Sat to pass the Holy Feast as one,
Where at the hour and day predicted
Their servant on the Octave bore them arms,
Flowing with alimony and fresh supplies
Vital for the keeping of their human lives.

But as they sat once more to eat their meal
Behold – upon their prow the foretold bird,
Throbbing with music from her outspread wings
As like from the vault of some mighty organ.
From which Saint Brendan knew at once her need
And waited with his crew upon her speech –
"Predestined, clement, omnipotent God
Standing now past all the circuits in your lot."

"Four points, four seasons wait, in perfect faith
For every path took wandering through your fate.
The Last Supper with your provender
This very fellow at your table here
Followed by this and that and every year
Easter on the dorsum of the beast
Then here with us until Pentecost
Passing forth by Albei and the Birth of God."

"Thus for seven anticipated years
Through listlessness and perilous trials
Come sought upon the blissful Land of Saints
Which you may inhabit for forty days
Before turning – to the island of your birth."
And flushed with salvation; grateful, praising,
Saint Brendan fell ecstatic to the earth
Fainted with his brothers in their turn.

To which the ancient venerable bird
Went again to her place upon her perch
And their servant at refection's end
"God permitting I will come once more with food
On the day the Spirit struck with light
To fright those apostolic heads with fire."
And from the saintly soul and all his men
He took his grace and went away again.

The Holy Abbot therefore made his stay
In full adherence to the ordained days
And with the consummation of the feast
He and his brothers siphoned from the well
To fill their casks – and fit their ship to sail,
But as they led their vessel to the sea
Behold afar, their forecast friend offshore
Steering with his burden to their port.

Wherefrom withheld he transferred their supplies
Then saluted them, returning to his isle.
The Holy Father with his brotherly crew
For forty days were carried on the sea
Where they saw at far, a beast of giant size
Spuming from its nostrils – looming on their lives
Compelled to death with such passioned haste
That it ploughed up all the ocean into waves.

And rushed before their sudden deaths
The unbelieving brothers sought the Lord
Crying for their lives – "God free us from here
That we are not devoured by this beast"
But the saintly Brendan comforted them
"Don't fret and cry and fright away your faith
God is our defender and will liberate
Every credent brother from this monster's face."

"Furthermore the Lord our God will stay
Every other danger in our way"
But as he spoke, their unheard end approached,
Outstripped by waves of such marvellous height
They made dread proportion with the brother's lives,
Who swelled and bested every crest with fear
Until their Captain raised his hands and said
"Liberate Lord your servants from their deaths."

"Just as you freed Israel's ancient sons
Jonah – the whale, Daniel – the lions
And David the boy from giant Goliath."
At which – in faith – the climax of his plea
They saw from the West another beast appear
Nearing past them to the passage of their fiend
And straightway violent – in life despising war
It savaged the monster with its burning jaws.

To this the elder spoke before his men
"Look my sons on our great redeemer
That even this heeds its heavens keeper
And as it goes so expect the end
Safe in the might of the Lord's defence."
And with these words – the sorrowful beast
That dared pursue these humble slaves of Christ
Cut to three parts, drifted from its life.

Softening, the second beast took leave
And they saw across a distance in the sea
An island dark, with each more massive trees,
Where washed ashore upon a treadless shelf
Forsook beside them – mutilated
A portion of the executed beast
"Behold, what now the sea has brought about
Once to devour us and now to be devoured."

And so the Saint instructing to his men
"Lift the boat and raise it on these heights
For we'll wait I'm sure a while upon this isle
Discover too some ground, a level site
To place our stores and set our tent beside."
Which setting out the Saint himself surveyed
And with the precept of the man of God
They lay their baggage ordered on the spot.

Beneath the shade the Saint arranged his men
"Take while you can brothers, from this swollen brute
Strip enough at least to last us three months through
For by nightfall beasts will devour its corpse."
And working near until the evening prayer
To haul the viands ordered by the Saint
The brothers asked at the end of the slaughter
"Well – but do we eat without water?"

"Do you think so little with such supply
That our Lord cannot a round provide;
Go then now to the South of the island
And measure from mouth of the fount you find,
Roots and herbs in rows upon the falls
Vying to be reaped with license to you all."
To which response they hurried in reply
And found each to be as the Saint described.

They waited therefore three months on the island
In forest bowers – dark with ocean storms,
And as the airs unbalanced on their heads
Blasting rains and hailstones on their tent
The brothers searched for the carcass of the beast
And coming near to where the corpse was laid
They found it gleaming, stripped of flesh
Bare but for the bones of its savaged breath.

Where took to confess to the man of God
"Father all of which you told us would be, was."
Which to their helplessness the Saint supplied,
 "I know well my men you wished to prove
Whether I knew, or if, even told the truth
Very well, another sign I give to you
Tonight that fish will wash upon the shore
And tomorrow will your sickly frames restore."

Which stalking by the dawn towards the beachhead
The wasted brethren saw what the man of God
Pre-warned – and setting aside, quickly hoarded.
"Brothers, be diligent and watch your stores
Cut some flesh to strips to dry in salt aboard;
Today the Lord will pacify the breeze
And ease for three more days the soothing sea,
For where will sail on gentle heaven's leave."

Chapter 9. The Island of Strong Men

With the days passed set as the Saint pre-told
His brothers packed their flasks of drinks aboard,
And gathered herbs and roots in bundled sheafs
For the priest their Father never took of meat
Which had held the breath of some helpless creature.
Plenished they sat aboard and raised their sail
Pulling outwards on a northern reach
Where they saw an island in the distant sea.

"Do you see that island there" Saint Brendan asked
Which affirmed informed "Its habitants are classed
With boys first, then youth, then third the oldest last
Which one of you will never journey further past."
To which over each; each brother queried
And saddened, persisting, the Saint relinquished –
"It is you Brother who will have leave to stay"
One of three that forced his passageway.

Closing soft they touched the island's shore
Planed flat, smoothed to the edge of the sea
Without a tree or any vital thing
To shift in the emptiness beside a breeze
But tract on tract of white and purple flowers.
There they saw the three troops as the Saint had told
Fixed apart at the cast of a sling shot stone
And spaced as such, across the meadows roamed.

Standing short a single troop let song
"The sacred march from strength to greatest strength
High before the God of Gods in Zion"
Flowing the next to voice the ceaseless rounds
The first troop, the boys, vest in shining white
Beside the youths in lines of violet
The third platoon of purpled dalmatics
The fourth hour watched the entranced ecstatics.

At the sixth hour, midday, the company
United, *"May God have mercy on us"*
Until the end, *"Incline unto my aid*
O Lord" and for the third Psalm the same
"I have believed" and for mercy again
At the ninth hour prayer after prayer after prayer
"From the depths," "Behold the good begun"
And *"Glorify Jerusalem and God."*

They chanted through Vespers, *"You are praised"*
"O bless my soul," "Children worship thy God"
Singing next the fifteen gradual Psalms.
With the finishing of the chant, at once
The island darkened with a swollen cloud
Of light far too bright and miraculous
Such that they couldn't see what hid
Before the inspissation of the mist.

But yet they heard the voices as before
Chanting without end the never-ending Psalms
Right until the Matins hours of pre-dawn
Where at once the new days mantras advanced
"Praise Lord of Heaven," *"Sing unto the Lord"*
"Praise be the Lord in His Saints" and after that
The Twelve Psalms set to the psalter's order
At which fresh and cloudless the morning dawned.

But as the first light lit, they sprung to song
Singing the Six Psalms, *"God have mercy on me"*
"O God – my God," *"Lord my refuge,"* *"All ye
Nations clap your hands,"* *"God by Thy name"*
"I have loved – because," Alleluia.
In communion *"Take up the body"* in song
Then the spotless lamb they sacrificed
"And the blood of God for everlasting life."

Thus the sacrificial party ended
Two troops from the youths platoon took baskets
Copious with fruit and placed them saying
"Take these fruits from the Island of Strong Men
Deliver our brother and proceed in peace."
"Hail brother" said the Saint, "and go with him
Who is called, what good hour was made of in
A man to merit to serve such men as this."

Then the Saint and all his brothers kissed him
"Son, record with love how God has set you down
Here, with such pure kindness – for go us pray."
Straight on he followed the two youths to their school,
While the venerable father grasped
With his companions, the sails to the sea.
Where at None he permit refresh his crew
With the Island of the Strong Men's fruits.

At lifting one the Saint remarked, "Never
Have I seen or read of florets so full"
They stood in equal measure to a large ball.
At squeezing one into an empty jug
The man of God poured out twelve ounces
Passing a full ounce to each brother
So that a single fruit for twelve days left
The brothers always with the taste of nectar.

Chapter 10.   The Gryphon and the Clear Sea

With some several days having finished passed
For three more days the Saint prescribed a fast
Where at the third night's close, a bird – behold
Flying powerfully towards the boat,
A branch in its beak from some unknown tree;
With large grapes clustered swollen at its tip
Miraculous red, dropped and let land
From beak of bird to the lap of saintly man.

Saint Brendan called his brothers to his side
And said, "Look up and take what God
Has set for us," a bunch of apple sized grapes
Which the man of God divided so that
Each had food for twelve days, one fruit per monk.
Again the man of God prescribed a fast
Where his brothers saw on the third day
Another island not long away.

This one was covered in every part
With plump thickets of boughs all bearing fruit
The same giant size as dropped by the bird.
So fertile the trees all curved back pregnant
Dropped to earth, resting fat their swollen skins
Of the same colour – unreduced red.
There was not one single un-expectant tree
On the whole isle or any other species.

Then the brothers set the boat in its bay
And the man of God stepped off alone
To walk this place that had such a smell
Like a homestead filled with pomegranates.
Which all the while the brothers in the boat
Waited for the return of the man of God,
But elated by the sweetness on the breeze
Somehow their fasts with reasons turned to feasts.

The Father meanwhile discovered
Six waterfalls watering some wild gardens,
Groves of herbs, and roots of all varieties.
Then the man of God appeared, returning
With the first flush of the island, and said
"Go up into the boat and find the tent
Be in comfort with this fruit that God has sent"
And forty days they fed beside the fountains.

Now the Saint himself and his beloved
Ascended into the boat, then after
The intended time with as much fruit
As all their little boat could carry,
Settled aboard, with sail spread-out and set
To wander wheresoever the wind would will.
Where navigating, they saw - a gryphon
In far off flight direct towards them.

Seeing this the brothers unable spoke
To the Saint, "To devour us comes that bird"
Who simply said in turn, "Don't be afraid
God is our accomplice here, as has done
Will defend us here again for this one."
Whence the bird stretched out its utmost claws
To grasp the Servants of God – but there
Above, the bird that brought the grapes to them.

Flying towards the gryphon with such speed
It set ready; combat quick to kill
And sickened, set back, plunged in defence
The bird yet overcame the beast – snatched its eyes
To which the eagle-lion, leapt to such heights
That the brothers could barely see it,
But their huntress chased until she killed him
And dropped it winging lifeless through the wind.

The brothers saw it plummet to the sea
Right beside their boat, as the bird returned
To its own home, Saint Brendan and his crew
Not many days after saw the island
Of the family of the Saint Ailbe.
It was Christmas time and they celebrated
With the brothers there the Birth of the Lord
Which fully finished days permit to board.

The venerable Father accepting
As he went, benedictions from the Abbot
And his community, then the same to them.
Circulating the ocean for such lengths
Of unkept time, save the pre-arranged dates
Of Easter and the Lord's nativity.
But for them in gentle restfulness retired
In the places and for the spans required.

Saint Brendan after some time had ended
Celebrated the feast of Saint Peter
The apostle, in his boat, founding
The ocean so clear they could easily see
Right down to the distant bottom beneath.
At this they gazed into the depths of the sea
And watched the many types of ocean beasts
Lying with ease in the sands of the deep.

They saw through so clearly they believed
They could touch with their hands the ocean's floors
So great too, was the clarity of the sea
They watched herds of beasts like flocks in pasturage.
And before them droves of such great number
They formed to one, connected end to head
A series of cities of circles resting
Inducing the crew to the Saint suggesting;

If the Venerable Father might see,
Whether possibly he could celebrate
The Mass quietly, even to himself,
So that those drowsing monsters of the deep
Would not hear and rise up to pursue them.
The saintly father smiled at this event
And told the men, "Of all we've seen on this trip
I'm most amazed at your stupidity."

"Why do you fear these beasts and not the king
Devourer of all the other fish
On which you sit, even barbequing it
Right there on its back, singing Psalms all these years.
Is not God the master of all the beasts
With Lord Jesus humbling everything."
Which this said the Saint began to pray
As loudly as his power could sustain.

The brothers with their eyes always on the beasts
Watched, as they heard the loudly singing voice
Rising to ring around them, from the sea floor
To the boat, so that the brothers could not see
Anywhere that was not a sea-beast frenzy.
Which yet did not come near the little ship
But swam until scattered to distant places
As the man of God fulfilled his graces.

Chapter 11.   Hell

Even now with eight days prosperous breeze
The Saint sitting with the sail fully raised
Could scarcely reach across the clear sea.
One day as he was celebrating Mass
There appeared a column in the water
Seeming not too far away, but yet
Before three days passed could they sail close enough
The man of God gazing on as they approached.

Straining to see as high as the top
They were too little to look up over
The summit of this mighty column,
As straight and tall as the sky itself
Covered by a canopy of the thinnest
Finest form, so delicate that the boat
Could pass right through its opened arches,
While all unknowing what creator made this.

To bring to being such a canopy
As strong as marble but curved as silver
The thick column, of clearest crystal;
So much so that the Saint said to his brothers
"Cast at once your oars into the ship
And the mast, and the sail, everything
Hold on to as we pass by presently
The fastenings of this canopy."

There was a space of a mile to the sides
Of the column, the wide contours too
Dropped in equal steps to profundity.
When they had done as asked by the man of God
He said, "Send the boat through this opening
So that we may see the great wonder
Of our Creator's natural mastery,"
Which at once inside surpassed what thought to be.

Entering further the ocean seemed
To vitrify and become perfectly clear,
And all that was below them they could see
From the column's base to the footings
Of the heights lying in the rock beneath.
The sun shone here too in this deep pool
No less bright than when on the other side
The Saint appraised the arch at six foot wide.

Then they navigated the whole day
Just to sail one part of the column
And felt equally cool from shade, and pleased
By the sun's heat, till the hour of None.
The man of God also measured the arc
Of the columns quadrant and found it
Fourteen hundred cubits and so likewise
They found each the same of the columns sides.

So for four days they worked the four angles
To measure this tower, and four days on
They chanced upon a fallen chalice
From the canopy's stock – a paten too
Carved from the colours of the column,
Both stood in a window facing South;
Which immediately apprehending
Saint Brendan, held the vessels saying;

"These are proclaimed by Jesus Christ our Lord
Miracles, and to bring to believe them more
Has given me to take this pair aboard."
To which at once the Saint instructed
The brothers to perform the divine office
So that after, they could refresh themselves
As they had no relief from weariness
Since seeing this sight, of water, food or rest.

By night's turn they took hold of their course
Navigating towards the North seas
Which when through the arches they raised their mast
And stretched the sail high, while the other brothers
Gripped till they were ready the canopy's sides.
As they stretched their sail a strong wind blew
Bearing them forwards, pressing them fast
With naught but grip the ropes and the rudder.

Thus eight days they were borne before they saw
A blackened island of burned out charcoal,
A slag pile, rocks without herb or tree
Full of workman's sheds and backyard factories.
To which the venerable father said to his brothers,
"Look brothers, I've observed that I'm anxious
Of that island – which long though landless
I would not go near it or let us land there."

"But the wind directs us straight towards its shore,"
And close therefore, within the flight of a stone
They sailed, and just some bounding echoes heard
The massive rushing bellows and thunder
Of mallets strike, to which Saint Brendan
Armed himself with the arms of the Lord,
Clasped head to chest and shoulders on four sides
With the impregnable cross he signed.

"Lord Jesus Christ free us from this island"
Where at the pause of his shortened prayer
The man of God beheld an island dweller
Exiting his forge with some needing look
Of some ordinary thing; poorly groomed
With hair and dirt burnt through to shining red.
Which when he spied the slaves of God's approach
Ran quickly back beneath the burning slopes.

The man of God rearmed himself and his men
"Sons, raise the sail as high as it will go
And pull the oars as hard as you can row
We can flee this land" and as quickly said
They saw again the sad barbarian
Shift by leaps with tongs towards to the shore
Gripping hot slag in a heavy heap
Which straightway heaved at the Saint in the sea.

He thrust the shot on the Saint's crews line
But it flew high out – a stadia too far
Making burning splashes where it struck
The sea like an erupted volcano
Smoke gusting and flashing from the ocean
As if spat upon a metal furnace.
And truly the man of God transferred them
A mile or more from the rocks descent.

At which act the island's every devil
Formed on the shoreline; lines of attack
Carrying singularly singular weights
Of burning rock which they hurtled at the Saint
In aggressive order, over one
The other, always dashing for more
From their furious workshops, where they lit
And simultaneously reappeared.

Perfectly ardent, the island burned
The whole place, blurred by their activities
The sea rolled like a mass of seething soup
Meatballs spattering in some cooking pot
Hung over coals and prodded with logs;
The whole day on they heard unnatural sounds
Screams from the island they couldn't see
And thick in their eyes the stench of burning.

Then Saint Brendan gave comfort to his monks
Saying, "Here, soldiers, in Christ's infantry
Shielded well with faith unfeigned, by fear
Heavily armed - truly spiritual
For we are in the border waters of hell
And so, stay vigilant; and act like men."
Then a land appeared as if a mountain peak
Held the clouds, with its cliffs upon the sea.

Floating with a string of smoke above it
The summit itself was fomenting hugely.
Immediately the wind changed its course,
With its new rush thrusting them forward
Where they would soon stuck crouched against the rocks.
But the shoreline's edge was so shear cut
They couldn't lift their heads to clear its top,
Just face on coal face, black cliffs of carbon.

The side of the shore rose unusually
Right angled and straight edged like a wall;
The last one of the three brothers, who stood
Exiles from the monastery that day
Climbed from the boat, to the shore, from the Saint
And paced with slow steps towards the cliff's base
Where he paused and whimpered saying, "Oh God
This is it; being wasted from your love."

"Yet I am without any power
To come back to you," which anyway
Clamouring, the brothers pushed off, panicked
"Have mercy on us God – God have mercy,"
Then halted as the venerable Father
Watched the unhappy man being taken,
Led by a multitude of demons, turning;
Shocked by his torture, already burning.

"Oh sad son what great thing did you hide
To be so unhappy; the end of your life."
Again they were seized by a firm breeze
Prospering them quickly to the South
But the apex stood a long time behind
The looming hidden wounded summit
Sucked flames back down, breathed out to the sky
Burning sea and land to an endless pyre.

Chapter 12. Judas

Thereafter Saint Brendan navigated
Southwards, where there appeared some sort of shape
A man almost, balancing on a rock
With a sack flapped before it, waving
The length of a cloak held between two forks
Spun of iron, and driven with every surge
Waves like a wreck in a tornado;
Which the crew disputed, sea-bird or wrecked boat.

The man of God overheard this conference
Inter-brethren, and quickly intervened,
"Cease contending without purpose in this spot
Direct the boat's course straight towards that rock."
But as the man of God approached, the waters
Stilled in a circle, as if nearly set
Where they found a lone man seated on the rock
Deformed, and thick with sodden gushing locks.

Until the next wave struck his foothold, swirling
Even up to the vertex of his head
And back down the naked rocks in waterfalls
Where the unhappy man sat fully exposed.
Sometimes even the flap of cloth would crack
Snapping against his eyes and his forehead.
To this the holy Brendan asked what sins
He did commit to sustain such penitence.

Which he said, "I am unhappy Judas
You know him; who made the worst of deals,
Not for my sake have I this place but for
Jesus Christ's ineffable mercy.
This term is not considered punishment
Rather an indulgence of the Redeemer
To honour the rising of the Lord,"
Which was indeed the day he was restored.

"When you see me sitting here I feel as if
I am in some sort of paradise,
Because of the continuous torture
That is so often in my future.
I am burnt up, heated through like an ore,
Lead liquefying in a crucible
Day and night in that mountain you have seen
Where Leviathan and his satellites teem."

"There I was when they devoured your brother
And when the inferno trumpeted
With glee as they always do when they take
Some impious soul; my cool relief
Lasts every Sunday, Vesper to Vespers
And too for the Birth of God right until
The Epiphany, Easter - Pentecost
The Assumption of the Mother of God."

"Afterwards and before, excruciating
With Pilate and King Herod in deep hell
Caiaphas and Annas too, I adjure
Intercede through the Redeemer of the world
To the Lord Jesus Christ and His power
That this relief could be extent till sun rise.
So the demons won't come to trade tonight
The fate I took for that terrible price."

"Let the will of God be done," said the Saint
"From night till morning none will harm you"
Then again the man of God inquired
"What is the purpose of this flapping cloth"
Which he, "This cloth I gave away one day
To a leper when I was a comrade
Of Christ, but yet it was not mine to ward
It belonged to the brothers and the Lord."

"Therefore, I don't get from it total relief
It slaps so often, my lapse to remind me
And the iron forks on which the flap hangs
I gave to the priests in the temple
For their pots to hang; and this slab of stone
You see me sitting on, I placed once
Over a trench in a public street
Under the pedestrian's crossing feet."

"This was before I was a disciple
Of Christ the Lord," where with the hour of Vespers
Overshadowing them, suddenly
An innumerable demon multitude
Darkened the ocean's daylight waters
And formed in a circle, loudly obtruding;
"Recede man of God because we cannot come out
To our associate here with you about."

"Nor dare we look at our prince in the face
 If we haven't returned his companion.
You've truly stolen our prize, so this night
You had better not attempt defend him."
"I do not defend," the Saint replied
"He is guarded by Lord Jesus Christ
Which I suggest with assurance this night,
Concede, you will have nothing till sunrise."

The advocating demon retorted
"In what just mode can you invoke the Lord
To save his very own betrayer."
"Hurry and go," replied the man of God
"In the name of our Lord Jesus Christ
You will do no bad to this man tonight."
And night, departing, the demons reappeared
In darkening swarms on the blue abyss.

With dire voices they emanated
"Dear man of God we come to curse your leave
Just as we did for your welcoming,
We have been flagellated this whole night
Whipped and whipped by our craving prince
With furious desire for his captive."
"To us" said the Saint "these are not pertinent
Your curses only worse your own torment."

"Don't you know that when you curse it blesses
And bless curse, so if you would, then bless us."
In some joint way the demons responded,
"For six days we will torture him twice as much
Unhappy Judas is about to feel,
The night which for you, just somehow passed us."
To which the venerable father spoke,
"But you don't have any power to do so."

"Neither you nor your prince are able
The power is with God," and added
"In fact I order you now in the name
Of our Lord Jesus Christ, your prince the same
Do not add to his excruciations
Ever again beyond their first gradations."
"But yet," responded, "is it possible
That you yourself are now the Lord of all."

"To thus sermonize and we obey?"
"I am," then saying, the man of God
"His servant in whose name I ordered
And I only have administration
In matters of His conciliation."
And harassing them they followed before
They no longer see where Judas clutched
But back with screaming force they plucked him up.

Chapter 13.   Paul the Hermit

Saint Brendan with his fellow soldiers
Sailed themselves into the southern oceans
Glorifying God in all – in everything.
On the third day there appeared a land
A tiny island, much further into the South.
Which seeing took straightaway to their oars
Nearing too quickly this faraway place
Where the Saint subdued the violence of their pace.

"Men – brothers, don't make your bodies weary
They are now over sated with labouring,
It is seven years since we left our homes
This Easter coming, but you will now know
A new sight, the spiritual hermit, Paul
Who on that island insulated
Without any corporal sustenance
Has survived, sixty years existence."

"And there too thirty years previous
He obtained his meals from some helpful creature."
When they approached nearer to the shoreline
They couldn't find an inlet anywhere
As the island's shear banks were extreme cliffs,
The whole place, exceedingly small and round
The maximum radius a stadia
Not a slip of soil on the plateaued faces.

In the wind just a cut of naked flint
Whose latitude and longitude if stood
Would meet at equal heights with its altitude.
To which circumnavigating the rock
They found a port so width restricted
It hardly wedged the boat's prow's tip inside it.
And the steep ascent from boat to tip
Steepened to join them and stricken up the cliff.

Then Saint Brendan told his men, "Wait here
While I return to you – it isn't licit
For instance, to enter this landing place
Without this island's man of God's good grace."
Then when their venerable father had climbed
Coming up to the summit of this island,
He saw two caves, face to face in a corner
Between them looking East towards the dawn.

In the shade of the mouth of one of the caves
Trickles pulsated from a fountain
As small and round as an offering plate
Running out from the rock of the doorway
Of where this man of God must surely dwell.
Saint Brendan neared the cave of the host
But came from the other a well-aged fellow
Out of doors, and stood up before him bowed.

Saying, "Behold how good and how joyful
It is for brothers to be blent to one."
At which the Saint with this subtle precept
Summoned the brethren from far below them,
To climb up the footholds from the boat.
The man kissed each one, sat him in a seat
And called each by his own name, which hearing
Yet the brothers watched still disbelieving.

As much at his dress as at his powers
Of prophesising, so odd was his habit;
He was completely covered by his own hair
From his head and beard and various places
All glowing snow white on account of his age,
With no other thing about him except
His own overwhelming head of hair
Which seeing the Saint, ungrounded in despair.

Inside him saying, "Ah me, who pretends,
Dressing in the habit of holy men
Many monks under me, under Order
And now we see a faultless angel
Untouched by any bodily vices
Although still living, sitting in the flesh."
To which the island's man of God replied
"Oh venerable father, what rare sights."

"In amount and quality have you seen
God meting out his miracles to you
Manifest to no other father.
Yet you say in your heart, you are a fraud
In a monks cloak, but see, you are greater
Than a monk – who must work with his hands
To labour with things and clothe his coldness
But you, fed and dressed from God's own larder."

"Feasting on secrets all these seven years
Sustaining too all your brethren crew.
And I, miserable, sitting like a bird
Perched naked but for my natural cover."
At this speech Saint Brendan questioned him
Asking about his advent to the isle
And for how long he had sustained such a life
To which the other, to the Saint replied:

"I was nurtured in a monastery
Saint Patrick's, and tended for fifty years
The cemetery of my brethren.
One day I was ordered by the deacon
To dig in a designated place
For the sepulchre of a brother.
But another more senior man appeared
Saying, "Brother, don't dig your hole here.""

"That is the place of another," Father
Said I, "Who are you," to which he replied
"You don't recognize me, your own abbot?"
"But Father, Saint Patrick was my abbot,"
"I am he – that is to say, yesterday
Migrated from life, and that here we are
At the very site of my grave itself,
Here, mark over there the other sepulchre."

"Don't tell anyone what I have told you
Tomorrow profess yourself instead
Direct to the coastline to find a boat,
Beached there for you to ascend, and be lead
Somewhere, bewilderingly faraway
Where you'll wait to part live that last of days."
The next morning stepped in obedience
To the sea as the saintly father promised.

I found a boat according to his word
I was taken at once on getting aboard
Navigating for three days and three nights
Until letting the sail flap and blow
Wherever the wind would will me go.
This rock then appeared on the seventh day,
Straightaway I went onto it and dismissed
My curragh where it came from with a kick.

Immediately I saw it coursing
With velocity, cleaving furrows
Cutting through waves on the steppes of the sea
Returning smoothly to its homeland.
I of course remained here, where at three
A sea-otter appeared to bring me lunch
A fish in its mouth fresh from the sea
With it also a little bunch of kindling.

It carried this between its front feet
While balanced on the other two behind it
Put right before me the bunch of firewood
The fish too, then raced back from where it came.
I smashed this flint rock with a piece of iron
Percussing it so as to make a fire
And made my meal with the fish and the kindling
Continuing each third day for thirty years.

This same small minister bore me the same
A fish to eat one third part each day,
And with great thanks I had no thirst at all
But on the day of the Lord, released
A paucity of water from the spring
That yet permit refresh my wishes
Allowed too, to fill my cup with water
To wash my hands in their natural saucers.

Then after thirty years I found this pass,
Hidden with two caves and a fountain
Here itself, and where then, sixty years I dwelt
With no other nourishments aught than what
From this font I've got, therefore all up
Ninety years in total on the island,
Thirty years of which was fed on fish
Sixty then in pasturage on this dish.

Fifty years before that in my fatherland,
Which adds to one hundred and forty total
Is all the time of my life, yet I wait
As I must in this mode, in my flesh
Expecting as promised my day of judgement.
Go on then to your homeland, take with you
Your vessels filled up spilling from this font
For forty days of sailing wait in front.

This will take you to Holy Saturday
From then to Easter Sunday and beside
All the Paschal days, where you have passed them
For the previous six years, and after
Accept blessings from your procurator
Setting out then to the Paradise.
Where you will be maintained forty days before
The God of your fathers turns you to your shores."

Chapter 14.   Paradise

Saint Brendan, therefore, took with his brothers
Benedictions from the man of God
Casting off for Lent, set sailing South again,
Voyaging for a total of forty days
From hither to thither, to and fro again
Their only meal the waters of the spring
Which they had accepted from the island
Each third day to portion their survival.

Yet they were refreshed without any hunger
Or thirst, luxuriating they endured,
Thus, according to the predictions
Of the solitary man of God, they came
Holy Saturday to their servant's island.
He ran to them as they reached the port
And with great gladness lifted each one up
From out of the boat with his own arms.

With the good works of the holy day
He appointed before them their repasts
And at Vespers climbed up with them in their boat
Sailing with the crew towards the whale
Which they saw at once in its first location.
All the night spent in chanting, praising God
Then with the morning masses finished with
Went off at once, atop Jasconius.

All the brethren who travelled with the Saint
Took at once to clamouring to the Lord,
"Hear us God, our saviour and our hope
Through earth's bounds and vastness of the oceans."
Saint Brendan comforted his brothers
"Don't dread bad things," he said, "assistance
For our voyage's close is imminent,"
At which the whale retook their course corrected.

Direct to the shoreline of the island
Of the Paradise of Birds, and rested
Until the Octave of Pentecost,
Passing this season of solemnity
Where the procurator said to the Saint,
Completing, "Ascend into your boat
Replenish your vessels from this spring
I will board as your companion on this trip."

"To lead, so you will find, which you would not
Without – the Paradise of the Saints."
And as they ascended into their boat
The island's birds all ranged to one in song
"Prosper, God our saviour, on your voyage"
Saint Brendan and the men who went with him
Then sailed to the island of their friend,
To pack the parcelled quantities dispensed.

Sea-rations for forty days voyage East
Their procurator at the prow himself
Every day directed to its closure.
Where by Vespers they were taken at once
Whited away by some blissful mist
So much so it was the most of their senses,
At which their procurator said to the Saint
"Do you know this mist upon the waves?"

"What is it," asked the Saint, in which reply,
"It is the cloud of light that covers the isle
Which for seven years you have desired."
Lighting within the pass of an hour
They re-awoke in unnatural whiteness
Resting in their boat upon the shoreline,
Where descending they saw a beautiful land
Wide and plentiful with fruiting plants.

Ever autumn, they drifted in their rounds
Never night-time, late afternoons – mornings
They tasted fruit and sipped drinks from the springs,
Forty days lustrous in oblivion
They wandered the isle, and couldn't find its end
A river flowing swift to its centre;
Saint Brendan watchful, conversed with his crew
"We're forbid to cross nor its hugeness view."

While they wondered a youth appeared to them
Greeting the crew with a great happiness,
Singling each monk out with his own name
Saying, "Greatly blessed and beatified
Are those that dwell within your family home
Praised eternally, for eternity."
With this he said to Saint Brendan beside –
"Behold the land you have sought for such time."

"You did not find it first for God desired
That you would understand his miracles
Strewn across the magnificent ocean.
So return at once to your native land
Carrying with you fruit from the island
And as many jewels as your ship can bear.
The days of your voyage are set to pass
You must sleep soon, alongside your fathers."

"After the rush of many laps of time
This land will be shown to your successors
During the age of the persecution
Of the Christians, having overcome them.
This wide river that you see flowing here
Divides this island, forever ripened
And all the time remains without decline
The light of the island – Lord Jesus Christ."

Thus truly they picked the fruits of the isle
And took precious gems of every colour
While the Saint took leave of their blessed friends
Their long-time procurator and the youth.
Navigating directly through the mist
They came at once to the Island of Delights
Held for three days in hospitality
Where blessed by all they left for home directly.

The brothers received him gratefully
Glorifying in God for the return
Of such a loved father, in orphanage
Helplessly deprived of his aspect.
Then congratulating the blessed man
The brothers on their caritas and love
And of all the happenings he could recall
He told to them the wonders of the Lord.

Amen

CPSIA information can be obtained
at www.ICGtesting.com
Printed in the USA
LVOW11s1033120717
541103LV00001B/5/P